D0014243

MAY 10 2007

Sheryl Swoopes

by Rosemary Wallner

Reading Consultant:
Dr. Robert Miller
Professor of Special Education
Minnesota State University, Mankato

CAPSTONE
HIGH-INTEREST
BOOKS

an imprint of Capstone Press
Mankato, Minnesota

Capstone High-Interest Books are published by Capstone Press
151 Good Counsel Drive, P.O. Box 669, Mankato, Minnesota 56002
http://www.capstone-press.com

Library of Congress Cataloging-in-Publication Data
Wallner, Rosemary, 1964–
    Sheryl Swoopes/by Rosemary Wallner.
    p. cm.—(Sports heroes)
    Includes bibliographical references and index.
    ISBN 0-7368-0780-2
    1. Swoopes, Sheryl—Juvenile literature. 2. Basketball players—United States—
Biography—Juvenile literature. 3. Women basketball players—United States—
Biography—Juvenile literature. [1. Swoopes, Sheryl. 2. Basketball players.
3. Women—Biography. 4. Afro-Americans—Biography.] I. Title. II. Series: Sports
heroes (Mankato, Minn.)
GV884.S88 W35 2001
796.323'092—dc21   00-010093

Summary: Traces the personal life and career of the Houston Comets' star forward.

Editorial Credits
Matt Doeden, editor; Lois Wallentine, product planning editor; Timothy Halldin, cover
    designer and illustrator; Katy Kudela, photo researcher

Photo Credits
Allsport USA/Todd Warshaw, 4, 7; Louis Capozzola, 17; Jim Gund, 18, 21, 22, 24;
    Marc Morrison, 26, 35; Otto Greule, 29; Al Bello, 30; Doug Pensinger, 32;
    Elsa Hasch, 38; Kellie Landis, 40, 42
SportsChrome-USA/Michael Zito, cover, 9, 10, 13, 14, 36

1 2 3 4 5 6 06 05 04 03 02 01

Table of Contents

CHAPTER 1

A WNBA Championship

It was September 5, 1999. Thousands of basketball fans packed the Compaq Center in Houston, Texas. The fans cheered as the Houston Comets and the New York Liberty played the season's final game. The winner would be the Women's National Basketball Association (WNBA) champion.

Some of the loudest cheers were for Comet forward Sheryl Swoopes. The crowd chanted "Swoooopes, Swooooopes." Sheryl did not want to let her fans down.

Sheryl Swoopes led the Houston Comets to the 1999 WNBA finals.

The Comets had won the last two WNBA championships. But Sheryl wanted to win this championship for a special reason. On August 19, Comets' guard Kim Perrot died of cancer. Sheryl and her teammates wanted to win another championship in Perrot's honor.

The Comets began the game well. Sheryl and teammate Cynthia Cooper scored 20 of the Comets' first 22 points. The team led by as many as nine points early in the game. But the Liberty came back. The Comets' lead was only 26-25 with 2 minutes, 30 seconds remaining in the first half. The Comets then scored seven consecutive points for a 33-25 halftime lead.

The Liberty cut the lead to seven points early in the second half. But the Comets held on to the lead by playing tough defense. Sheryl and her teammates held up their arms as the final seconds ticked off the clock. The Comets won the game 59-47. Streamers fell down from the ceiling as the players celebrated their third consecutive WNBA championship.

Sheryl and her teammates took an early lead over the New York Liberty.

About Sheryl Swoopes

Sheryl Swoopes has played for Houston since the WNBA began in 1997. Sheryl is among the game's best and most popular players. She is one of the most well-known female athletes in the world. She has won basketball championships in high school, college, the Olympics, and the WNBA.

Sheryl also is successful off the basketball court. Girls and boys throughout North America wear Comets' jerseys with her number, 22. She does not make as much money as professional men's basketball players do. But she earns money off the court by endorsing products. She appears in advertisements for companies such as Nike. Nike even named a line of shoes after her. They are called "Air Swoopes."

CHAPTER 2

The Early Years

Sheryl Swoopes was born March 25, 1971, in Brownfield, Texas. Brownfield is in western Texas. It is about 40 miles (64 kilometers) from Lubbock.

Sheryl lived with her mother, Louise. Her father left their home soon after Sheryl was born. Sheryl has two older brothers named James and Earl. She also has a younger brother named Brandon.

Sheryl's family did not have much money. They could not afford a car or vacations. Sheryl could not often buy new clothes like many of her friends did.

Sheryl was born March 25, 1971.

Learning the Game

Sheryl did not always want to be a basketball player. She wanted to be a nurse or a flight attendant. She also dreamed of becoming a cheerleader. But Sheryl never became a cheerleader. Her family could not afford to buy a cheerleading uniform.

Sheryl learned to play basketball at a young age. James and Earl enjoyed the game. They played whenever they got a chance. Sheryl began playing with her brothers when she was 7 years old. Her brothers and their friends did not want her to play. They did not think a girl could play basketball with boys. They sometimes would refuse to pass her the ball. They also would play rough with her. She often had to stop playing because of scraped knees and elbows.

But Sheryl's brothers sometimes helped her learn to play. They taught her to dribble and shoot. They saw that she could be a good player. She was already among the tallest children in her class. Some of her classmates

Sheryl earned the nickname "Legs" because her legs were so long.

called her "Legs" because her legs were so long. Sheryl learned quickly by playing against her brothers. She had to be fast and tough to play against the older boys.

At first, Sheryl's mother did not want Sheryl to play basketball with the boys. She wanted Sheryl to play in the house. But Sheryl played anyway. She wanted to prove that she was good enough to play with the boys.

Sheryl learned quickly that she had a great deal of basketball talent.

Sheryl joined a girls' basketball team when she was 8 years old. The team played in the Little Dribblers' league. Sheryl was one of the best players on her team. She led the team to the Little Dribblers' national championship tournament in Beaumont, Texas. But her team lost in the championship game.

I don't worry what people think. Back in junior high, the guys would tell me, 'You can't play basketball.' That gave me all the more incentive.
—Sheryl Swoopes, AP, 8/1/97

High School Success

In 1985, Sheryl began attending Brownfield High School. She played basketball and also was on the track team. She also worked hard on her studies.

Sheryl became more serious about basketball during 11th grade. She wanted to earn a college scholarship after high school. She knew that she could not afford to go to college without a scholarship.

Sheryl led Brownfield to a 29-8 season record. The team advanced to the state championship game. There, they played Hardin-Jefferson. This team was the best in the state. Hardin-Jefferson had finished the season with a 35-0 record.

Brownfield fell behind early. The team trailed at halftime by a score of 25-19. But Brownfield played better in the second half. Sheryl led Brownfield to a comeback victory. She scored 26 points and had 18 rebounds in the game.

Sheryl led her team with 26 points per game during her last year of high school. She also averaged five assists and 14 rebounds per game. She was named an All-American. She also was named the Texas High School Player of the Year.

Choosing a College

Many colleges offered Sheryl scholarships while she was in high school. She accepted one from the University of Texas in Austin. The Texas Longhorns had a powerful women's basketball team.

Sheryl left for college in the fall of 1989. Austin was about 400 miles (640 kilometers) from Brownfield. Sheryl quickly became homesick. She missed her family. She also missed her boyfriend, Eric Jackson. Sheryl returned home only three days later. She decided that she could not live so far away from Brownfield. Many people told Sheryl she was making a mistake.

Sheryl decided to attend South Plains Junior College in Levelland, Texas. South Plains was only about 30 miles (48 kilometers) from

Sheryl wanted to stay close to home during college.

Brownfield. Sheryl played for the South Plains Lady Texans basketball team. She led the Lady Texans to a 27-9 record during her first year. She was named a junior college All-American.

Sheryl's second year at South Plains was even better. Sheryl was named the Most Valuable Player of the Western Junior College Conference. She also was named National Junior College Player of the Year.

CHAPTER 3

The College Years

Sheryl chose to attend Texas Tech after she finished her two years at South Plains. Texas Tech is in Lubbock. It is close to Brownfield. At Texas Tech, Sheryl could play against the best college basketball players.

Texas Tech had a good women's basketball program. But it was not as good as the program at the University of Texas. Many people thought Sheryl had made the wrong decision when she chose to attend Texas Tech.

Sheryl was an immediate success at Texas Tech.

Immediate Success

Sheryl was immediately successful at Texas Tech. The team won the Southwest Conference championship during Sheryl's first year there. Texas Tech never had won the conference championship before. The title earned the team a chance to play in the NCAA tournament. Texas Tech lost in the tournament to Stanford University. Stanford went on to win the NCAA championship.

Fans and sportswriters began to notice Sheryl. During one week, Sheryl scored 56 points in two games. *Sports Illustrated* magazine named her the women's college basketball player of the week. After the season, Sheryl was named to the NCAA All-American team.

1992 Olympic Trials

The United States did not have any professional women's basketball leagues while Sheryl was in college. Women had few opportunities to play organized basketball in the United States after

Sheryl returned to Texas Tech after she failed to make the Olympic team.

college. But Sheryl had one goal. She wanted to play in the Olympics.

Sheryl tried out for the U.S. team during the 1992 Olympic trials. She made it through the first sessions of the trials. She felt confident that she could earn a spot on the team.

Sheryl's dream did not come true. She hurt her ankle during one of the tryouts and could not continue. She did not make the team.

Instead, she rested her ankle to prepare for her senior season at Texas Tech.

Senior Year

Sheryl led Texas Tech to another successful season during her senior year. The team again advanced to the Southwest Conference finals. There, they faced the University of Texas.

Sheryl wanted to play especially well in the championship game. Many of the Texas fans and players remembered her. They wanted to prove to Sheryl that she had made a mistake by leaving their school. But Sheryl did not let Texas prove her wrong. She scored a career-high 53 points. Texas Tech celebrated its second conference title.

The conference championship put Texas Tech back in the NCAA tournament. This time, the team advanced to the Final Four in Atlanta, Georgia. Sheryl wanted her family there to see her play. Her mother and brothers drove 19 hours from Brownfield to Atlanta. It was the first time Sheryl's mother had traveled outside the state of Texas.

Texas Tech won the Southwest Conference title in both of the seasons that Sheryl played there.

CAREER STATISTICS

Sheryl Swoopes

WNBA Per-Game Statistics

Year	Team	Games	Points	Rebounds	Assists	Steals
1997	HOU	9	7.1	1.7	.8	.78
1998	HOU	29	15.6	5.1	2.1	2.48
1999	HOU	32	18.3	6.3	4.0	2.38
2000	HOU	31	20.7	6.3	3.8	2.81
Totals		101	17.3	5.6	3.1	2.40

CHAPTER 4

New Challenges

Sheryl's future in basketball was uncertain after college. She could not earn money by playing professional basketball in the United States. She would also have to wait three more years for the next Olympics.

Air Swoopes

Sheryl found another way to earn money. The Nike shoe company was looking for a female athlete to endorse their shoes. The company asked Sheryl if she would be a spokeswoman for Nike. Nike paid her to wear Nike shoes and clothing. She also would appear at events to endorse the company.

Sheryl hoped to continue playing basketball after college.

Nike's most successful line of shoes at that time was called "Air Jordan." These shoes were named for basketball star Michael Jordan. Nike wanted to make a line of basketball shoes for women. They called this new line of shoes "Air Swoopes."

Sheryl worked alongside Jordan to endorse Nike. They made appearances together. Jordan even asked Sheryl to work at one of his youth basketball camps. One day, Sheryl and Jordan played a game of one-on-one for the campers. Sheryl took an early lead over Jordan. But he came back to beat her 7-5.

A Trip to Italy

Sheryl wanted to keep playing basketball. She decided to play professional basketball in Europe. Many talented women's players from the United States played there. Sheryl did not want to leave the United States. But she thought that she had to try professional basketball.

Sheryl agreed to play for Bari. This team is based in Italy. She played and practiced there

Sheryl played basketball whenever she could after college. She wanted to keep her skills sharp.

for three months. But she quit after just 10 games. Sheryl said the team was not honoring the contract she had signed. She said the team was not paying her as it had promised. She also missed her friends and family.

Sheryl returned home. She worked as a bank teller in Lubbock during the day. At night, she exercised. She played basketball whenever she could. She often played on pick-up teams with men. In June 1995, Sheryl married Eric Jackson. Sheryl and Eric had dated since high school.

The Olympic Team

Sheryl kept working to improve her basketball skills. She prepared to try out for the 1996 women's Olympic basketball team.

Sheryl's hard work paid off. She was named to the Olympic team in May 1995. She began training at the U.S. Olympic Training Center in Colorado Springs, Colorado.

Sheryl and her teammates went on a world tour before the Olympics. They played games throughout North America and the rest of the

Sheryl was named to the 1996 Olympic women's basketball team.

world. The team won all 60 of its games. Eric traveled with Sheryl on the tour. He helped her deal with her homesickness.

The Olympics began July 19, 1996, in Atlanta, Georgia. Team USA easily advanced to the gold-medal game. There, it faced the team from Brazil. Team USA was in control from the beginning. Sheryl scored 16 points in a 111-87 victory. She and her teammates had won the gold medal.

The WNBA

Team USA's Olympic victory increased interest in women's basketball in the United States. The National Basketball Association (NBA) began a league for women. The new league's name was the Women's National Basketball Association (WNBA).

Sheryl was one of the most respected women's basketball players in the world. WNBA officials asked her to play in the league. Sheryl agreed to join the Houston Comets as a forward. The WNBA's first season would begin in the summer of 1997.

Sheryl led Team USA to a gold medal in 1996.

Sheryl did not begin the first season with the Comets. She was on the team's injured list. But she really was not injured. She was pregnant. Sheryl gave birth to a son four days after the Comets began their season. She named the baby Jordan. He was named after Sheryl's friend Michael Jordan.

Sheryl worked to get back into shape. Six weeks later, she played her first game for the Comets. She played only five minutes. But the crowd stood up and cheered loudly for her.

Sheryl played more as the season went on. The Comets were the best team in the Western Conference. The team made the playoffs and advanced to the championship game. There, the Comets beat the New York Liberty 65-51. They became the first WNBA champion.

Sheryl and the Comets were successful again in 1998. They finished the season 20-10. They advanced to the championships. This time, they played the Phoenix Mercury in a three-game series. The Comets won the series 2-1 to earn their second WNBA championship.

Sheryl joined the Houston Comets during the first season of the WNBA.

CHAPTER 5

Sheryl Swoopes Today

Sheryl remains one of the WNBA's most popular players. She is one of the most recognized female athletes in the world.

Continued Success

Sheryl and the Comets continued their success in 1999. Before the season, Sheryl and Eric divorced. Sheryl assured her teammates that the divorce would not affect her play. She predicted that 1999 would be one of her best years yet.

Sheryl is one of the most recognized female athletes in the world.

> It seems like when I think things can't get any better, they get better. I have a lot of people to thank. The one thing I said, if I won the MVP trophy, I wasn't going to cry.
> —Sheryl Swoopes, AP, 8/17/00

In July, fans voted for their favorite players to play in the WNBA All-Star Game. Sheryl received the most votes from the fans. The WNBA awarded her the first-ever All-Star "Top Vote-Getter Award."

In August, Sheryl had 14 points, 15 rebounds, and 10 assists in a game against the Detroit Shock. This made her the first player in the WNBA to record a triple-double. The Comets won the game 85-46.

The Comets finished the 1999 season with a 26-6 record. They faced the Liberty in the finals. They won the series 2-1. It was their third consecutive WNBA championship.

Sheryl had her best season in 2000. She led the league with 20.7 points and 2.81 steals per game. Sheryl's performance earned her the 2000 WNBA Most Valuable Player award. She also earned the league's Defensive Player of the Year award.

The Comets faced the New York Liberty in the 2000 WNBA finals. The Comets won the first game 52-50. Sheryl scored 31 points in

Sheryl is among the best players in the WNBA today.

the second game. The Comets beat the Liberty 79-73 in overtime. Sheryl and her teammates celebrated their fourth straight WNBA title.

Beyond Basketball

Sheryl has interests outside of basketball. In 1996, she wrote a children's book titled *Bounce Back*. This autobiography tells about Sheryl's childhood and her basketball career.

Sheryl also travels around the United States teaching people about Respiratory Syncytial Virus (RSV). Thousands of children die from this disease each year. Sheryl teaches parents to watch for the symptoms of RSV. Symptoms include high fever, cough, and breathing difficulty. Sheryl believes Jordan may have had this disease as a baby.

Sheryl is not sure how long she will play in the WNBA. But she wants to find a job in sports when she retires. Sheryl has said she might like a job in sports broadcasting after her basketball career is over.

Sheryl wants to continue working in sports after she retires from the WNBA.

Career Highlights

1971—Sheryl is born in Brownfield, Texas, on March 25.

1978—Sheryl begins to play organized basketball.

1989—Sheryl is named Texas High School Player of the Year.

1991—Sheryl is named National Junior College Player of the Year.

1992—Sheryl is named to the NCAA All-American team.

1993—Sheryl earns NCAA Player of the Year honors; she leads Texas Tech to its first NCAA championship and is named MVP of the Final Four.

1994—Texas Tech retires Sheryl's jersey number.

1996—Sheryl wins an Olympic gold medal as a member of the U.S. women's basketball team.

1997—Sheryl becomes the first player to sign with the WNBA's Houston Comets; the Comets win the league's first championship.

1998—The Comets win their second WNBA championship. Sheryl is named to the All-WNBA First Team.

1999—The Comets win their third WNBA championship.

2000—Sheryl is named the WNBA's Most Valuable Player; the Comets win their fourth WNBA championship.

Words to Know

autobiography (aw-toh-bye-OG-ruh-fee)—a book in which the author tells the story of his or her life

contract (KON-trakt)—an agreement between an owner and a player; contracts determine players' salaries.

endorse (en-DORSS)—to support a product by appearing in advertisements

scholarship (SKOL-ur-ship)—a grant of money that helps a student pay for college

symptom (SIMP-tuhm)—a condition that shows a sign of a disease; a sore throat can be a symptom of a cold.

To Learn More

Burgan, Michael. *Sheryl Swoopes.* Women Who Win. Philadelphia: Chelsea House Publishers, 2000.

Kelly, J. *Superstars of Women's Basketball.* Female Sports Stars. Philadelphia: Chelsea House Publishers, 1997.

Ponti, James. *WNBA: Stars of Women's Basketball.* New York: Pocket Books, 1999.

Sehnert, Chris W. *Sheryl Swoopes.* Awesome Athletes. Edina, Minn.: Abdo & Daughters, 1998.

Swoopes, Sheryl, with Greg Brown. *Bounce Back.* Dallas: Taylor Publishing, 1996.

Useful Addresses

The Basketball Hall of Fame
P.O. Box 179
1150 West Columbus Avenue
Springfield, MA 01101-0179

Sheryl Swoopes
Houston Comets
Two Greenway Plaza, Suite 400
Houston, TX 77046

Internet Sites

CBS Sportsline.com—WNBA
http://cbs.sportsline.com/u/basketball/wnba/
   index.html

ESPN.com—WNBA
http://espn.go.com/wnba/index.html

Sheryl Swoopes—My Official Web Site
http://sherylswoopesdirect.com

WNBA.com—Sheryl Swoopes
http://www.wnba.com/playerfile/
   sheryl_swoopes.html

Index